GRAINS OF SAND IN THE WIND

THE POEMS

OF

FRANCIS HARTLEY, IV

1962 – 2012

GRANOS DE ARENA EN EL VIENTO

Printed in the United States of America

F. H. IV IN PARIS   LE LOUVRE

Frank Hartley, Poet To Read At Library *Grains Of Sand In The Wind*

It has been many years since Frank Hartley has read his poetry to a public audience. On Sunday, June 25, he will return to the public library with a reading at Boothbay Harbor Memorial Library. This reading is the first event of the new Reading in the Great Room program at the library.

A Yale educated historian who began writing his poetry while at university, Mr. Hartley's work has been likened to the works of Wallace Stevens. His works have been praised as among the best in our time. As a young man, Mr. Hartley had the pleasure of meeting Robert Frost and discussing the process of writing poetry with him. His travels around the world and his facility with three languages have informed his distinctive collection of works. Moreover, his many years of living in relative solitude have added depth and nuance to his poetry.

Mr. Hartley will be reading from his acclaimed volume, *Grains of Sand in the Wind*. At the reading, he will discuss his personal experience with the creative process of writing poetry. He will also touch upon the central theme of most of

FRANK HARTLEY

his works, his lifelong fascination with the meaning and the nature of time. At the reading there will be an opportunity for questions and comments from the audience.

The Memorial Library is proud to reintroduce this fine poet to the Maine community. Join us on the 25th at 3 p.m. in the Great Room. This program is not best suited for very young children. For more information call the library.

"You have a gift for capturing moving insights in **exactly** the right amount and choice of words that, I think, would stir envy in many of the best-known writers in the history of this language…I have since worked hard to increase the density of my writing, in an attempt to come closer to the magnificent intensity and sense of mood, as well as oneness of 'message and letter', which you can bring off with bewildering perfection."

Niall MacKenzie
Ottawa, Ontario

"He had obviously thought about the essence of poetry and expressed his thoughts about it very clearly and with a remarkable economy of words which illustrated one of the elements of poetry he presented."

Robert O'Brien
Washington, D.C.

1974

THE FARM   KITTERY POINT

"SWEETIE"

NORTH HATLEY   QUÉBEC   CANADA

MONTRÉAL   ON THE MOUNTAIN

Francis Hartley, IV spent his early years in Kittery Point, Maine. He attended Phillips Academy, Andover. Mr. Hartley later graduated from Yale University.

Mr. Hartley lived for many years at "The Farm," Kittery Point, Maine.

Mr. Hartley has travelled around the world extensively. He has lived in Spain. He has lived for a number of years in Québec, Canada.

Mr. Hartley lives with an abiding reverence for the natural world of birds and animals, the sea, the trees, the fields, and the marshlands.

To My Readers:

I hope that my last words and my last chapter have not yet been written. But the muse is an independent spirit. She visits me without warning and she is inclined to leave in the same way. My poems begin during my years at Yale University. Thereafter certain poems express reflections during my travels to many countries. A few poems I wrote in Spanish. They are followed by their English translations. Many later poems attempt to reveal the nature of Time.

Francis Hartley, IV

1986

I have never sought profit nor fame. I write only for the pleasure of writing.

I hope that my written works will stand on their own and speak for themselves in the years which follow me.

My muse tells me to continue writing.
Father Time is always at my back.

F. H. IV

September 2012

She gave the mountains to us

That we drink the crisp clean air

A gift to man

An earthly heaven

A refuge from despair.

F. H. IV

September 1962

Wild winds blow hard

While ice cakes squeak

On the creek

As I watch from the hill

And no one speaks.

Not even you.

F. H. IV

WINTER AT THE FARM   1962

Two Old Men In March

I was there in the village shop
When an old man came walking in.
"It won't be long now, will it, George?"
"No, guess not," was all he said.
I wondered what they meant.
Perhaps George had fishing on his mind
Not long before the blue fish fly.
A fishing hat was on his head.
I think his friend meant the rush
And business from the summer tourists.
Their lives near spent they may have meant
Soon enough they will both be dead.

F. H. IV

1963

That oak tree over there
It knows despair:
The sooty filth of city air.
But oak trees need not cry
For April brings new hope to the eye
With last year's woes but the slits in leaves
Which are now blown far away.

Farther and farther away.

Even they will come to rest
On the breast of an empty clear
To bring new life to the air
And the pleasure of innocence.

F. H. IV

April 1963 on the New Haven Green

Yes
I am a Sin Thesis
Of a finger's snap
And a sagacious grin.
I am a surf bubbles breaking
On a beach's brim.
I am vain.
I am modest.
I am complex simplicity.
That I am I know
Though I wonder
What I be.

F. H. IV

21 October 1964
Yale

Beach Birds

Does he have a plan of flight
Or a map inside his wings
To keep from going South in Spring?

The best place to watch from is
A beach's end
Just after the break of dawn
When a beach bird's shadow
On the moon blanched sand
Announces his destination.

F. H. IV

June 1966

Funny how I struggle

To ascertain the truth

Midst the mass of ambiguous men.

If there is a heaven

I hope I will not go there then

I would rather wander the cosmos

Or become grass by the sea.

F. H. IV

1967

Joe comes home
A gypsy man
At dinner for all to see.
Everyone is cheerful
Dutifully
Like wasps being etherized
Within their nest.
Piano laughs
Relief at last.
Joe was lively and sad.
I ate and I drank
And I watched.

F. H. IV

1968

I have howled
At stiff white collar clergymen
Wearing rough beaten leather boots
Who, drinking whiskey,
Discuss life with their colleagues
And, from time to time,
Seem almost human.
They are like actors
Discussing acting
While trying to be real.

F. H. IV

1969

And life seems freak you say
Like something in between
Our chips of joy
Fractured sunset folly
And blended endless dream
Hearts sparked
Then wet by foam and mist
I can not talk now
Nor do you hear me well
Wait Ulysses
Please wait for me.

F. H. IV

1969

I have argued
And talked
And listened.
Travelled, seen, smelled and stared:
Men, mountains, pubs and plains
Deserts, women and streets
I have heard.
I have been rained on
And I have been scared.
And novels bore me.

F. H. IV

Mount Kilimanjaro, Kenya en route to
Pretoria, South Africa
1970

I have teased Death

Now I run

Lest

He catch me.

F. H. IV

16 November 1970

Look way beyond a blind man's eyes

And try to hear the silence there.

Then know the silence

And let it speak.

F. H. IV

16 November 1970

Seagulls

I have often watched seagulls
And wondered what they knew.
This gull walks
This beach
This way
And struts
And stops
And seems to say
To me
"This is my beach
And this is what there is."

F. H. IV

May 1975
Kennebunk Beach

Love Poem

It came to be
We met on a beach
We danced with the moon
And soon
We sang to the stars
Together.
You looked at me
So I caressed the sky
With mine eyes and soul
From above the sea.
Then I ran with the wind
Farewell to the earth
But before I left her
I said thank you God.

F. H. IV

1975

La Ville De Québec

After long journeys
Endless faces
Countless café places
I have come back to rest again
With the best of my brain belonging in one place.
You ask me if I could understand you.
You raise your hand to say, "No."
Yet knowing I do understand you.
Where you slept
Your mind-journey's past
Thoughts of what you have wrought
And what you had hoped to do.
Oh, of course, I could not know,
You defend yourself in saying,
That same dry throat gasp of fear
When he died
Or she left
Or the baby screamed
Its life snuffed out
When alone was what you were
And all you knew.
How could I understand, you say,
As if I had not been there too.

F. H. IV

1975

When the dark of the mind's eye

Is pierced by light

And the sun shines down

Upon Machu Picchu

You will know that your heart's alive

And that the sky there

Caresses you.

F. H. IV

1976
Bogotá, Columbia

When the clouds of the soul

Are obscured by night

And the moon brights up over Frenchman's Bay

You must know where you belong

And that the world leaves you

On its way.

F. H. IV

1976
St. Thomas, Virgin Islands

"Molly"
Conversation With A Dog

This is life,
Is it not, Molly?
We eat
We sleep
We wag our tails
We cry
We run
We jump
We keep our hope
We die.

F. H. IV

13 April 1976
Moody Beach

The light flashes as the comet passes overhead

Before the mind's eye beholds what is lost

Like the illusion of childhood returned in a dream

Gone as one enters the glaring morning light

Shone down upon the streets of men

And disappears into the mass of traffic

And heartless faces

Masked in emotion you can not read.

F. H. IV

10 November 1980

A Winter's Poem

Roar you rageful winter roar

You and I have clashed before

December and the leaves have gone

The wind scowls down

The ice cakes speak

Gone are all the hoary ghosts from here

Just I, the wind, and the creek.

F. H. IV

1 December 1980

In the wake of my anger's death
Betrayed by your wretched hubris left alone
And splattered by long ago
I watched your puerile rage
Just as it spermed from your infancy
And placed you on a stage.
I would rather see you confirmed
By your frothful patterned madness
Like the ill-scented bitch dog
Who was lost in the sun.
Tits apart with nought to suckle
When it is over you crawl to your shack
And try to sleep.

F. H. IV

1980

Like the early dwellers of Camargue
The Sphinx still scorns the barren wind
And piercing grains of parch dry sand
Flown down that haunted morning hour.
The vulture seeks its own reward.
I stand as from the riverbank
The world gave up its time
The moon has lost its fire again
The sun grows red at dawn.
I tell you that we spoke before
That day a thousand years ago.
Your smile has changed for me its tone
It now becomes you more.

F. H. IV

7 January 1981

23

When I tell you that we'll speak again
In another part of space my friend
Can we talk of things Elysian then?
How white the snow
The sound of wind
The breath of leaves
A song of dreams
And how they all come back again.
When the dove soars high above the hawk
We'll talk of magic circles
And worlds of love and how they touch
Our rainbows red are woven beds
For fairies dancing overhead.

F. H. IV

19 January 1981
Harvard Square

I live alone in the demimonde
Of shadows, the sunrise and sounds of the sea.
You speak to me of freedom
And how they notice who you are
The terror in your eyes diffused
As you take your café table.
You fly to Paris within the hour.
Then take a night train
To the inner harbor of your mind
And find you can not leave behind
Your weighted image of yourself
And how the cosmos needs you.
Shrouded in the fog you stand
The viewpoint of an ostrich.
My feet are swallowed in the sand
As the seagull chick makes his plea
And breaks his nest
And struggles on the beach at last.
The sun is warm upon my back.

F. H. IV

15 August 1981

To The Memory of Anwar Sadat

Have you ever lived a moment of your life
Separate from the race?
A moment of isolation splendid
When god is a sardonic sulking face
Gone wild in your mind and replaced.
Sublime in your silence
Knowing you would never trade your madness
For his reason.
Nor will you find his children clean
Untarnished, all his little ones, in time, I mean
He punishes them in dreary lives of inchoate shame.

F. H. IV

1981

Last night I walked out
To the old red barn
Trying to decide exactly
Where the best place would be
To hang myself
And shut the doors.
The silence was broken by the plaintive stirrings
Of an abandoned barn bird chick
In search of his nest and family.
I waited in the cold.
The night was dark.
This morning the sun came up
And my friend came out singing.

F. H. IV

1981

Herbie's Trip

Here comes Herbie the bicycle man
Whose wizened face and faithful course
Are known to those who love him.
He picks his bottles with an eagle's care
And drops them in his basket snare.
He knows from where
His survival comes and
How to get there
Back and forth along Route One.

F. H. IV

25 December 1981
Route One, USA

28

The Crow I Missed

Hello old crow what do you know
Are you the one I tried to shoot that day
En route to school the age of eight
Who stared at me to say I missed the point?
The continua of life
Are the images of youth.
The sounds are terse of this old knight
He guards his castle in the sky.
One could do worse than measure time
And watch the birds go by.

F. H. IV

1 January 1982

Hello my pine trees dark and deep

My children enchant me.

You smile at me

My fortress tree

As a bright spot in the cosmos.

F. H. IV

1982

Pensamientos

Let me speak to you of freedom
All you forlorn fools
Monkeys and sheep and all you creatures rused
By the game of life and your sense of
Self importance.
Why did you not heed the lesson of Ozymandias
When he warned you long ago
Upon the desert sand?
You could have seen your visage there,
Shattered, and saved yourself some time.
What you perceive to be is not to be
Your monuments of time and faith
And what you think you save you waste
Credit cards and Cadillacs and a ticket to the grave.
I do not hate you America
Though I fly from you, far away,
That I can love you from a distance
And upon my high ground stay.
Please come with me, my friends, and fly
Of this you can be sure:
Time waits with patience at your door
And poets do not lie.

F. H. IV

1982

To All My Brothers And Sisters

Let me take you on a ride with me.
Descend the miasmas of your mind
To where you can breathe again and
Undeterred remove your burden
Of who you are and what you seem.
Where are you now Eva Perón;
Why did she leave her children there?
Did you hear about Bobby Seale?
Even the birds were singing scared.
You sold your tears and insolence
For your booze and the little fence
Around your house on Main Street since.
Goodbye to indignation
Now you have it won
The greatest union race I mean:
It took away your face
And left you there without a scream.
Come to the edge of Saturn's ring
To the archipelago of dreams
Come faced to see your world as one
And time as nothing
And how a star becomes the space.

F. H. IV

1982

In the stillness I can hear the purely quiet
And I can hear the laughter of the cities far away
And see the dim lit shanties
Along the beach shore rim.
The fog is fickle and will not stay.
The night is redolent with circumstances
While the rain cloud passes.
In the darkness I can see
The fire in your eyes.
The Phoenix bird takes back his flame
And rising from the ashes
Still longs to see you
One more time again.

F. H. IV

1982

The Phoenix bird of ancient Egypt knew

Risen from the windswept ashes

That while the golondrina searches

The swan already knows.

F. H. IV

1982

The sunrise lights the desert red
A camel brays the news
The smoke is thin meandering
Above each simple doorway
While the village hardly stirs.
Like the Sphinx who waits
And will not smile
The silence speaks and answers time
With frequent satisfaction.

F. H. IV

9 June 1982

Qué serena es la madrugada

A la playa por la mañana

Qué fresca es la arena

Al tocar a mis pies

Yo puedo ver tu cara

Ahora en la sombra

Los pájaros vuelan arriba.

F. H. IV

1982

How serene is the dawn

At the beach in the morning

How cool is the sand

Upon touching my feet

I can see your face

Now in the shadow

The birds fly above.

F. H. IV

1982

Descended From The Apes

There is a local gangster
The cheap and common small town kind
Flashing smiles like a crocodile
Who speaks in a cultureless nasal twang.
Like the ancient Sardinians
And venal scoundrels of the past
He waves a flag bandana
Claiming to be a patriot
No other place to hide.
As a wily public servant
He has purchased the police.
The town hall is like a brothel.
Behind its red façade
Are those who dwell there often
Like monkeys caged in a whorehouse yard.
Whether fool or fooled
No one will admit these truths.
But he knows
And he knows I know.

F. H. IV

1982

The life has gone from summer's whim
The light dims through the autumn leaves
The ocean sprays the spirits in
The squirrels climb their trees
The moon is full with winter fury
The river still on course will freeze.

The moon face beckons me to go
And now the hasty river slows.

I tried to speak with you before
Who had not the time to listen
The darkness lights the night
Of this journey into time
I doubt that I will stop again
Along this riverbank of mine.

F. H. IV

1982

I hope that you can understand
The ordinariness of man.
The world which lies before you
With a coaxing child's caress
Is really a place of players
Like monkeys mounted on a jungle stage.
Sometimes they even feign their rage.
And how they love to climb your wall.
While grains of sand accumulate
I watch potentates rise and fall.

F. H. IV

25 July 1983

The Old Red Fox Returned

I just saw a fox at the bottom of the hill on the old stone bridge.

This is the first time I have seen a fox at The Farm since the first time, the first day, when I arrived here as a child on 4 July 1950. At that time, I saw a fox running in the meadow beyond the stone bridge. For many years, I have waited for him to return.

The old fox was still red with some brown coloring. He has a light, yellow-white undercoat. He took his time on the stone bridge. It is that kind of deep cold winter day when little moves. I believe that the old fox has been forced to search and forage at a further distance than is his custom.

He was in no rush when he looked up here at me, startled but not afraid in the bright sun which shone down upon the snow all around him. He left the stone bridge after ten minutes there and he sauntered onto the frozen pond below, then back along the banking where he disappeared before reaching the well.

The old red fox is brave and wise and he is no fool.

F. H. IV

Saturday 21 January 1984
11:15 AM

For your heart's abandoned passion

And for the sadness in your eyes

Seek out a paradigm of stars

Where the sky will kiss the sea

With laughter there in place of awe.

Watch how the rain reveals the sun

Without fear or rancor.

F. H. IV

1984

The day is moody
The snow is melting
The old red fox returned.

The sun has taken leave
But not for long
It hides behind a cloud.

The crows are quiet
The marsh birds mellow
They seem reconciled.

I can see the fog come through
The pine trees swaying
The old stone bridge is mute.

F. H. IV

3 February 1984

Salida De España

I made my exit from the dark

And saw my shadow on the sand

My expectations left behind

I find at unappointed times

Like the heron making dances

The delight of unspent chances.

F. H. IV

1984

Let the world know that you spent time there
Tell the people that among your words
Were tears and songs and accolades
For their dreams unanswered.
Shout it if you must
That the rain clouds passed us
And that we both have gone.
I saw you first from a beach's dune
And later in a window flash.
A city street bus quickly passed.
It matters not that we met in glances
When you looked at me
Our eyes did dances.

F. H. IV

18 June 1985

María Teresa Lorente Bardoz
1967

I entered your open door late in the night.
The candle flickered as you led me up the stairs.
For a month I watched your dances
And drank your wine and ate your flan.
You smiled at me to stay and plotted my return.
I had time to give away at twenty three
And then I left red earth of Spain
Not knowing but not to see your face again.
Fifteen days or fifteen years.
They are not the same.
I did return Teresa.
The door was closed
The windows shuttered
The same Majorca street smell
And pungent summer air
But you had gone and no one knew your name.

F. H. IV

15 July 1985

46

Cuando nos nacimos

Comenzamos a morir.

Tan corta es la vida

Que siempre yo sé que

El tiempo es nada.

Meintras tanto es todo.

Yo no soy más que

Un grano de arena

En el viento.

F. H. IV

1 septiembre 1985

When we were born

We began to die.

So short is life

That I always know

That time is nothing.

Meanwhile it is everything.

I am nothing more than

A grain of sand

In the wind.

F. H. IV

1 September 1985

Por fin
El tiempo
Hará menos
Aún la luz del sol.

———————————

In the end
Time will dim
Even the light of the sun.

A veces me siento vagando
Entre las olas del mar.

———————————

At times I feel myself wandering
Among the waves of the sea.

F. H. IV

14 September 1985

49

You may find yourself
At the edge of the sea.
Shrouded yellow sea grass sand
Browns and orange hues are hushed.
Stand and breathe upon the dune brow.
Take the time to look around
And let yourself be calmed.
Do not fear the silence
Nor the reminders whispered
Of your solitariness.
Neither will you need
To think yourself important
Or embellish who you are
If you are one.

F. H. IV

16 September 1985

Here comes the rain

The pain has gone from here again.

Soon falls the snow

And time to think things Elysian.

If you were scared

The day you found yourself alone

Just remember

That time will change you more than once.

F. H. IV

3 October 1985

In the cold and silence

Of a still December day

Under heavy clouds

When the ground is hard

Before the first snow flies

Knowing the moon is full

I can smile at you

Though you are far away.

You will not see my smile.

F. H. IV

1985

She escapes her bourgeois life
As a beatnik in the evening
And sips her wine alluringly
At her sidewalk table
On the Rue Saint Denis
Pretending to be free.
One could as logically seek
Refuge in a sinking lifeboat
Or be an actress in a zoo.
I would rather give thanks
To a god ill perceived
For the herons and ducks
Who live by the sea.

F. H. IV

1986

Tu vida es una ilusión

No seas engañado

Al mismo tiempo

Debes guarder tu fantasía.

Your life is an illusion

Do not be fooled

At the same time

You must keep your fantasy.

F. H. IV

1986

Hello Death all dressed in black
Why do you mock me with an owl's eye
Why not turn back
And why do you cry that way?
I have no fear of you
Nor of your Omnipotence.
You may make me dust and vapor
And take these words away.
Try to take my laughter too
So serious are you.
I will howl at you ceaselessly.
I would not want your burden.

F. H. IV

1986

Forgive me world of people
If I surprise you.
I have spoken to the wind
And have been advised by Father Time.
There are places where I have been
In the crevices of the mind.
What you perceive as real
Is really your confusion.
I would rather dine with the devil
Than with the bourgeoisie.
My journey is often friendless
But it is never boring.

F. H. IV

1986

To The Tempters

He who teases fate
And tempts disaster
Seeking notoriety
By going up in a rocket
And expecting to return
Should know that he will receive his reply
From the heavens
And he must not blame the cosmos.
He will pay for his arrogance.
The cosmos restores its balance.

F. H. IV

1986

The Time Of My Life

I swam in the ocean Indian
In Africa in the evening.
I saw pyramids in the desert
As the dawn broke overhead.
I watched tyrants and their troops at Entebbe.
Later they were thrown from power.
The London nights grew loud one time.
The streets in Paris were quiet.

I hope you have seen the snow fly
While knowing that the Spring would come
And that the orange trees in Iberia
Bring new lovers out each year.

F. H. IV

1986

After the long night flight
It was raining hard when the jet
Touched down on to the tarmac wet
A West Indian island rain
Warm and soothing upon my face.
Inside the airport was quiet.
Only the clatter of a distant bar
Broke the early morning lull.
Shadowy figures pushed their brooms
Along the speechless floors.
Then on the road the palm trees blew
They danced and bent in the wind
The air was rich and redolent
And full with expectation.

F. H. IV

1986

I am in a time of absence
Rolling clouds and faceless peasant people
When less is more
Where pride is removed
To a place of peace
Without fear of death
Nor need of praise.
The crows are my friends.
We live in the trees.
I am one with the wind
And the sand and the grass.
At my back is a nameless sadness.

F. H. IV

1987

The Other Side Of The River

When I go to the other side
Will I be met by Hyades
And say farewell to solitude?
Will I be led to a place benign
To listen to the flute?
I would like to hear its echo
Not haunted by nostalgia
Between the sand dune and the sea.
I hope to smell the salt air
Laced with rose and pine.
Beneath the moon I will delight
In shining bougainvillea.
I will thrive on scented flesh message
And the magic of splendid legs entwined
Of the sea nymphs who live at the river's side.
 I will fill my cup from time to time
With quiet conversation.

F. H. IV

15 May 1988

I have always loved you
Even when I cursed you.
I have caressed you with my joy and tears
My pine trees and shore rocks and ducks in line
Proud ~~cows~~ Crows, seagulls and fragile birds in vines
My fields and leaves and moody skies
The coming and going of the tides
The setting sun of Autumn days
The solitude of snow bound ways
The charged blush of Spring's emotions
And Summer's head long rush to fall.
I have loved you all.
And when I leave you, parts of me,
Please know that I have loved you
As well as a lover can.
Can we not meet again?

F. H. IV

28 October 1988

To Those Who Follow Me

When I have gone
Watch over my fields and pine trees please
Take care of my birds parentally
The ducks are familial as they stay in line
The seagulls are gentle when they hover like lovers
The herons are fickle about their dances
Sometimes they succumb to fear
They do not return each year.

Just now I watch a blue jay sway.

Remember my crows; they are not understood
I knew their ancestors at childhood
They are my orphans with memories
They rule their domain which they have claimed
And they even know they should.
Imagine the secrets of the owl
Behind his blinking scowl.
Have patience and he may tell you
A tale of the truth of time.

The tides will come in then leave again.
They are an eternal rhythm.
Be weary of man's arrogance
When he tries to explain this whim.

Have you ever in your life entered within your soul
And known the feel of flight there
And your kinship with your friends with wings?
Have you wondered why you had not stayed there
And learned of higher beings?

Just try to stay aloft next time
Seize the moment before it flees

And drift, let go, and float alone
And say farewell to worldly things.

F. H. IV

1 May 1989

I am both bold and silent
But before you judge me
Remember that my ventures
Are fraught with the hope of flight
No less than that of the lumberjack
Whose vanity at each fallen tree
Is shaken by the sight of saplings —
We are veiled nearly everywhere —
And who knows that somewhere
Is another world.

F. H. IV

6 September 1989

Do not tell me of time
And how it flies.
I see rockets in the skies.
Some yesterdays ago
I rode my bicycle along a country road.
The autumn afternoons were cold.
Free of care though pensive for my age were I
The time was slow.
All I needed were my dreams in the wind
And a bright sky.

F. H. IV

21 January 1990

I remember the air in the late afternoon
In the month of June
On the beach at Talamanca
On the island of Ibiza.
This was the place of a young man's dreams.
I savored the sounds of the old town's narrow
streets.
I walked among their sleepy sun bleached walls.
The pensión guests took their naps by the sea
Their windows open to the breeze.
There were simple stirrings at the bar
And samples of Hierbas Ibizincas.
I drove the horse and carriage along the beach.
My hopes were high, my spirit free.
I drove them fast.
Teresa waited for my return.
We were never again to meet.

F. H. IV

1990

Are you well, dear woman?
We may not meet again
Because of where I am going
And where you have been.
I am the last to leave the beach each day.
All the people are in a hurry.
How they scramble to their stories.
Of echoes I am free.
The future has arrived for me.
The evenings are plagued with promise
Sometimes they haunt me
When they twist and are melancholy.

F. H. IV

1 March 1990

You ask of Joe Dimaggio
And where he went
And how to know
While even Joe can not speak
Nor tell you of the telling of the years
Where we all were
Which we now have spent.
Not a tear remains.
You do remember the infant
On the beach that time
The mystery of the mist
And the joy of waves sublime.
Sand cakes and castles in the sky.
That child is you
No matter what worldliness you claim
Or if you failed at fame.
The rose, it has not changed.
But you are wiser now
And closer to the end.
There are fewer seasons left to play.

F. H. IV

1990

Like chasing windmills on a broken horse

Like the lily white on the lily pond

Which blooms before the winter casts its shadow

long

I wish with life to take a chance

And dance this one last time

Before I have gone.

F. H. IV

22 May 1991

You can recognize that man hating
Seemingly sensitive and refined
American middle class female kind
From very far away.
They have pretty feet
But bare feet in sea side restaurants
Are still not chic.
They will not look you in the eye
A man like me I mean.
She talks louder and licks the ears
Of her loathsome lesbian friend.
She is the one with blonde hair and usually taller.
You know she has never been laid
And even more wicked than her partner.
It never occurred to that awkward pair
That a man could travel in Africa to watch the birds
And love the baseball back at home
And listen to Pergolesi and the flute.

F. H. IV

19 July 1991

71

The Last Winter

When the light of the río branches
While the owl's eye askances
We will then have better chances
To see the dove fly free.

I lie awake to see the night
The spirit flees the morning
I await the movements of the deep
The pink horizon is laughing.

The people are squawking
While the seagulls are talking
In the midst of a mischievous wind.

F. H. IV

1991

I am become Time
And I am here now with you.
I am the chronicler of your time and times.
Do not be shy nor fear to speak to me
And laugh and live your lives and lines.
Fear not as an ingénue
Because you know I heard you long ago
Before you made your plaintive sound.
I mean that first time when bound
Only by the caress of your mother's breast
You still knew even then that you would come to
hope
For a future joy fantastic
Whispered by when
To be one day a man or woman.

F. H. IV

7 January 1992

Yesterday I transcended Time

In the Springtime of this new heartfelt laughter.

I was glad in the lilac air

Along the sea road bend.

And I no longer hurt spiders.

I set them free.

F. H. IV

28 May 1992

First I came to the land
Like a child running to the sea.
Then the land came to me
Like a tree the ground
Like the leaves a tree.
We attached ourselves and grew
The land I beneath the sky.
The chapters of this tale
Thus wove with the waves and the sand of time.
Then the land wanted to let me go
And I could not let go.
The clouds, like my hair, turned gray one day.
Then I wanted to go
And the land would not let me go.
In the end we are one
And we are at peace.

F. H. IV

1993
Age 50

The clouds now move past me fast.
They are not decided.
They are like footpaths
In a path I can not stop.
I look deep into the disspissite lines
Behind my pines
My vision more blurry
Though not today
My insight more weary
And there is nothing but snow all around me.

I looked for you all my life.

I never found you.

F. H. IV

2000

I went to the mountain tops to look
Even Kilimanjaro far away.
I searched the barren desert sands of Egypt
Hoping to find her there one day.
The cities and their streets
Left me solitary and alarmed.
I laughed and wept through the seasons
And I seemed to play my life away.
Until one cold night
Under bright stars by the sea
And a sky deep purple.
My heart was warm.
Then like an apparition long hidden
She appeared to me.
There was my loved one
In my arms.

F. H. IV

3 March 2001

Running Time

I ran with the toros in Pamplona

You never have seen such a sky.

María waved to me that morning

We had not the time to ask why.

The many checkered faces

Along the side lines waited.

F. H. IV

1 January 2002

Cat In The Night

The rain drives hard
Upon my window pane.

My old black cat and I.

Mon cher petit chat dort.

In a warm café, pretty woman,
You explain why I do not know you.

Mi querido pequeño gato duerme.

I now mourn not for you
Nor for the day
But for my cat in the night.

F. H. IV

15 July 2002

If you have ever known
Greatness in your life
When history and hope were one
If you have ever climbed
To the peak of the mountain
And gazed down over
To the other side
Your eyes rolling down over
To the other flora
You can now
Come down
And calm yourself
At the river side.

It is over.

F. H. IV

1 May 2005

Hurrah For The Wind

Hurrah for the wind
And for the Farah Diva
And for all my friends
Nearly every where.
We are now part old
And still part children.

Pronto salimos.
Escuchen amigos.
Ahora vivamos.

We may be gone soon.
Hear me my friends.
Let us live fully.
There is no time to lose.

F. H. IV

1 May 2005

El Nueve De Abril 2005

Tus lágrimas me importan
Aunque ellas son pequeñas
Porque para mí
Tú estás fina
Siempre dedicada y buena.
Dá me tus besos
Yo te daré los míos.
Quédate al mi lado.
Siempre estaremos juntos.
La vida me pasa
Ahora sin duda.
Gracias Dios.
No me querría otra.

F. H. IV

1 mayo 2005

The 9th of April 2005

Your tears are great
Although they are small
For me
You are marvelous
Always loyal and kind.
Give me your kisses
I will give you mine.
Stand by me.
We will be together forever.
My life is passing me fast now.
This is clear.
Thank you God.
I do not want another life.

F. H. IV

1 May 2005

May Day

What great laughs

You and I have had

And you are still not mad.

When you place

Your eyes in mine

I find

A kindred spirit there in time.

I am glad.

F. H. IV

1 May 2005

I can see in full sight
The mystery of the night
And the early morning light

Whether to be together

While the birds take flight.

The owl howls
What I might.

You see
The sea
As I see the sea.

You are listening
Shimmering.

Life gleams for me.

F. H. IV

7 July 2005

Leave before

The other people

Under the steeple.

Be you good to your friends

And have glad amends

At the height of your life

While the juice still flows.

F. H. IV

7 July 2005

I may not be

Long here

With you

Laughing

Please people

Just speak

Say something.

F. H. IV

7 July 2005

I know you are there

Somewhere.

We have not yet met.

Wait for me.

I will wait for you.

Our kisses

Will mingle

Together

Forever.

F. H. IV

7 July 2005

Do not cry for me

Take my hand

I am

The man

From Argentina.

I still have time

I have not yet found you

My perfect

Woman

Lover.

F. H. IV

7 July 2005

Hello Wind

Come in

Come in Wind

When you want to see me.

I want to see you

When

You want to see me

Wind.

F. H. IV

7 July 2005

My Cat

My cat

Sweetie

My cat and I

Are nuts

About each other.

Love at first sight.

We stay up all night.

She sleeps on top.

We would marry

But we cat not.

F. H. IV

28 July 2005

My life

Is

A dance.

Askance

Are my heroes

I do not yet know

And rainbows

Where

I have yet to go.

F. H. IV

16 April 2006

My cat

Some times it seems

Is

Such

A

Lazy

Dog.

F. H. IV

16 April 2006

I have been to the peak
Called Aca Dame.

Pretty woman on the sand dune
I know your name.

Come be with me.

Come soon.

As fast as a whistle
Like a butter cup
In bloom.

F. H. IV

16 April 2006

The End

The blazing yellow leaves
Are nearly green
This autumn afternoon.

Like a cat chasing her tail
I throw snowballs in the wind.

The lions who loved you
May walk around your grave one day.

The distant fog and faro bell
Sound their haunted beckoning knell.

F. H. IV

16 June 2006

In the beginning
I mean when I asked you
The moment I was born
To give me light
You gave me light.
In my life
The dark swept over me
Like a Su Nami
Like when she left me
My first love
I remember you.

This autumn afternoon
I blow you kisses in the wind.

I think of you my love.
You have forgotten me.

F. H. IV

1 October 2006

I can not own you

Such a beauty

As the sea.

The sea can see

I can not own you

More than she.

Pretty woman

On the sand dune

I let you go now.

Be not

Be reft

Of me.

F. H. IV

1 October 2006

Cuando
La lluvía
Te toca
Tu cara

Cuando
Tu amas
Las gotas

No importan
El frío
Ni el viento

Tú puedes
Estar cierto

Que todo está bien

Con el mundo

Y con tu alma.

F. H. IV

5 febrero 2007

When the rain
Touches your face

When you love the rain drops

No matter the cold
Nor the wind

You can be certain
That all is well

With the world

And with your soul.

F. H. IV

5 February 2007

The Nap Not Taken

I climbed the apple tree
Secret hiding place
Brave of me
Spring time afternoon
The age of three.

I refused to sleep.

I wanted to hear
The whistle train.

The distant sound.

I wanted to know
One day
The many places
Where I
Like the whistle train
Would go.

F. H. IV

21 March 2007

At this early
Morning light
I can see the sun
Trusting through the pine trees.

My color birds start singing
En chanting and speaking
And tweeting.

My cat is at my feet
Yawning and waiting.

Now, my friends,
Be lifted up
To know another day.

F. H. IV

12 September 2007

Halloween

In my sleeping dreams
Each night is Halloween.

My cat licks my face
And awakens me.

She tells me it is time
To play.

My realities are many
My nightmares torment me.

When I awake
It is always better
Sunny or rainy.

When I meet my end
I hope to be at peace.
And no more Halloweens.

F. H. IV

23 November 2007

In the purring
Of the wind
You can see the cat there
Left behind.

Like the momentary Nasdaq
There is not the time to cry.

Their chances are like children
Playing marbles out of fear.

I like the lines
In my faces.

They trace me back
To many places.

In the end
I am at peace
My dear old cat and I.

F. H. IV

21 December 2008

The red dawn fights
My early morning light

While wisdom casts me
In a prism.

This exultation I have found
Is bound to spiral
And let me down
Deeper
In the frosty winter.

F. H. IV

1 February 2009

After the roar and the shouting
The clouds passed fast
Even cheering
They are still there waiting.

You can go down there now
Upon the plains
Without fearing

How the yellow triangle
You and she
And I were feeling.

Into the rain barked trees
The fox is disappearing.

F. H. IV

20 March 2009

Try to eschew
The epitome
Of ordinariness.
Stay away
From those
Who
Like the froth
And receding tides
Backing down
Upon the pebbles
Whether you know it not
On this dark night
Always
Hold you back.

F. H. IV

1 May 2009

My Life As A Cat

My days are sunny and rainy
Wintry and windy.

I am older than The Sphinx
Her days are sleepy and sandy.

My father will feed me
He thinks he owns me
I keep him down to earth.

I always surprise him.

On the night
When the moon is full
I sit on my window sill.

The world lights up before me.

F. H. IV

3 July 2009

Breakfast in Spain

Like a waiting landslide
I have hurried
Through this life of mine.

Fewer days remain
While your whisper
In my ear is clear.

You are there now
Standing in the rain.

Brave bird you are.

I miss you Ana Cases.

We won the lotería.

Many kisses in the wind.

F. H. IV

1 August 2009

I went to the darkest of Africa
Before the tourists came.

In the North East of Uganda
One night asleep by the side of the road
I was awakened by thoughts of Idi Amin.

I felt alone.

Next day the elephants raced behind me
Like tremulous showers of thunder
Along the darkened pink swept paths.

My thought was simple then:
Just bring me home.

On a rainy sea side café day
The pretty woman's mouthful smile
And legs and eyes
Focused me away.

F. H. IV

10 September 2009

"Eyely"
My One Eyed Squirrel

I met "Eyely", a one eyed squirrel, on the mountain in Montréal just up from where I lived on "Le Chemin De La Côte Des Neiges" not far from the Olmstead Bridge. "Eyely" and I met each autumn afternoon in 1996, the same time and place in the late afternoon sun.

"Eyely" often climbed on my shoulder and licked my cheeks and ears. He leaped into my imagination. I watched "Eyely" jump fearlessly from the tops of birch trees with skill and joy even with the frosty winter coming on. He liked to show off and why not. "Eyely" especially liked jumping from one distinguished white "bouleau" birch tree to the "chêne rouge" oak tree not far away – but too far for me to jump. "Eyely" knew he was different from the others and stronger and wiser. When "Eyely" licked my ear, the strength of our bond was clear. "Eyely" always came back to me. Then one day "Eyely" went away.

The day when "Eyely" left, "Eyely" took me with him and we soared above all the people and all the trees.

F. H. IV

27 June 2010

How we go there
You and I
Like homeless crows
Beneath the sky.

The colden clouds
Above our ears

Will hide our fears
For now
And from frosty
December years.

F. H. IV

1 December 2010

You can fly down there now
And alight upon the hill.

Do not look back
With an apple in your pocket
This sun filled autumn afternoon.

My cat
She hesitates.

My squirrel climbs her tree.

My life now is my beauty

My beauty beside the sea.

F. H. IV

30 May 2011

The beginning of the caboose
Of my life
Is the circle of the circles
Like the circles I made yesterday
And the day before
And fifty years before.

First I saw you.
Then I missed you.
I miss you now.

When I saw you there
The marshlands were bright and mellow.
Some days were outstretched unending.
Today the Spring has come.
This robin is singing.

F. H. IV

1 June 2011

YORK HARBOR, MAINE

This mother bear is there
In the splash back of the icy river flow.
She had cradled her cubs in her paws.
She lost her chase and her chance
At the undaunted moose and her suckling young.

The old moose cow was unshaken
Startled in the morning sun.
They moved on to bray and laughter.

This V long geese band
Is a family flying South.
They will stay there
To their completion
After their colored autumn rush.

These eternal rhythms
Let my spirit hush.

F. H. IV

4 April 2012

The middle of my life is the age of the ages.
I remember on a beach line
That time I saw you there circumscribed
In a bikini on Talamanca in Ibiza.

You were recumbent like fruit drops
Like a lucullan life
And you were prepared to dine.

Last night you were coming hard
Like a whirlwind
As in a wet dream
Coming like the wind
Thrice swept back upon your door.

She loves you now
She ripples in your pond.
The chapter of these chapters
She will love you never more.

F. H. IV

23 July 2012

When the day comes
And you remember me
Just say that I did laugh with you
And that I kept my secret well
How I sang to the stars
On the banks of the Nile
I danced with the rain in Palma
The beginning and end of time were one
Riding horses on the beaches
In Spain in the evening.

F. H. IV

20245248R00076

Made in the USA
Charleston, SC
03 July 2013